Colors of Thanks

Fall Verses & Seasonal Art

Coloring Book

Note:

Due to the paper limitations with online printing, it's important to place a blank piece of thicker paper behind each page while you color to prevent bleed-through. This way, your art will stay crisp and clean!

Share your art work:

We would absolutely love to see your artwork! Please tag us using #Biblelampcoloringbooks across all social media platforms to showcase your amazing creations!

⊙ Instagram: Bible.lamp

ⓣ TikTok: Biblelamp

THIS BOOK BELONGS TO:

FALL BREEZE AUTUMN LEAVES

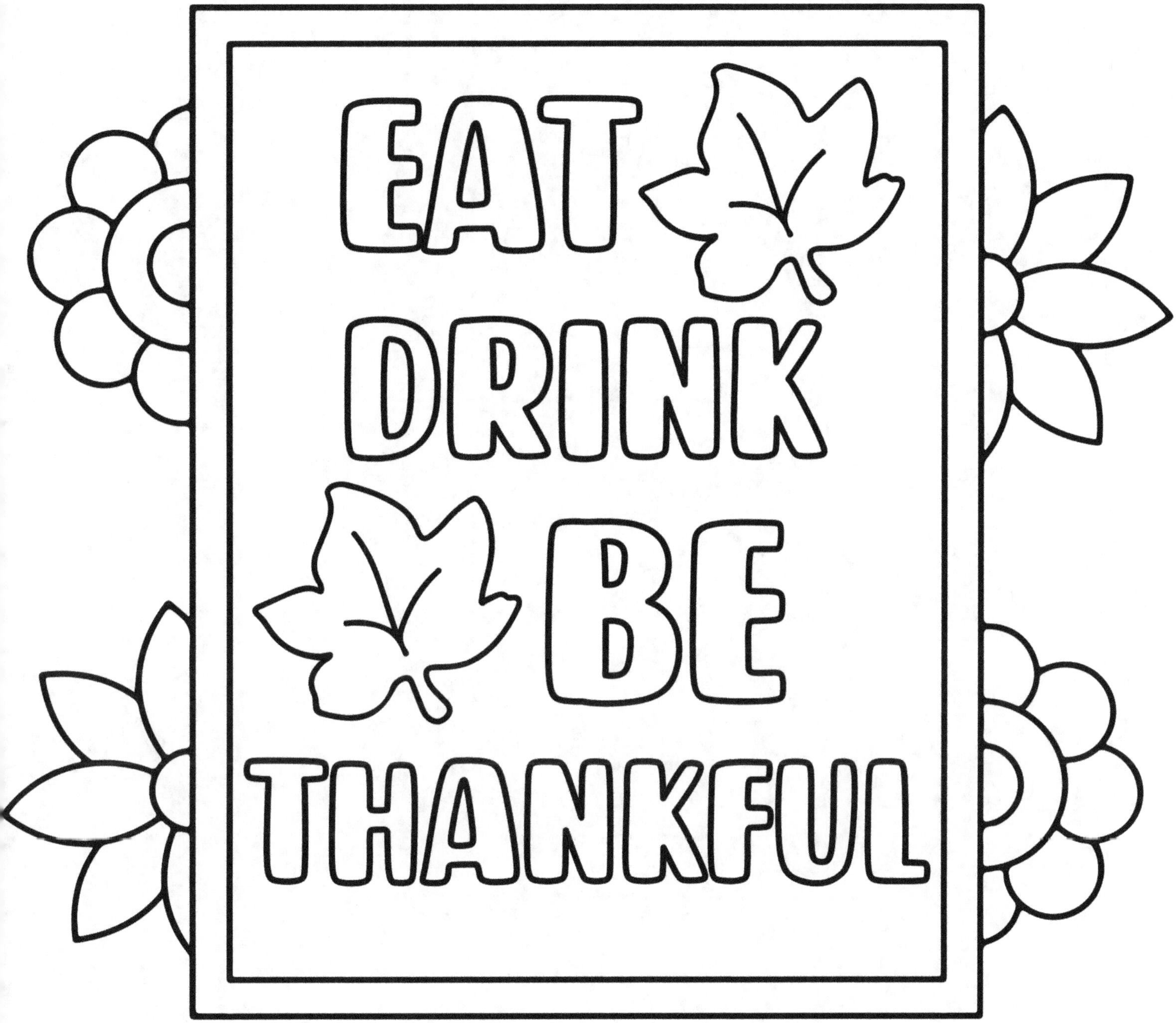
EAT
DRINK
BE
THANKFUL

THANKFUL
GRATEFUL
BLESSED

I YAM WHAT I YAM

FALLING LEAVES RISING SPIRITS

EVERY DAY SHOULD BE A DAY OF THANKS